40 Prayers of Victory

"But thanks be to God, who gives us the victory (making us conquerors) through our Lord Jesus Christ" (1 Corinthians 15:57)

by

Pastor Beverley Marrett

authorHOUSE®

AuthorHouse™ UK Ltd.
500 Avebury Boulevard
Central Milton Keynes, MK9 2BE
www.authorhouse.co.uk
Phone: 08001974150

© *2007 Pastor Beverley Marrett. All rights reserved.*

No part of this book may be reproduced, stored in a retrieval system, or transmitted by any means without the written permission of the author.

First published by AuthorHouse 12/19/2007

ISBN: 978-1-4343-1683-7 (sc)

Printed in the United States of America
Bloomington, Indiana

This book is printed on acid-free paper.

All Scripture references used is taken from various versions of the Bible listed below:

    New International Version – (NIV)

    New Living Translation – (NLT)

    New King James Version – (NKJV)

    Amplified Version - (Amp)

    King James Version – (KJV)

Acknowledgements

First of all I want to thank my dear Heavenly Father, precious Jesus and the sweet Holy Spirit for enabling me to serve the body of Christ with this project. He is the author and the finisher of my faith. He is the Alpha and Omega the beginning and the end. All the glory goes to God.

I want to thank my dear husband who encouraged me to "push the boat out" and publish a book, you are the love of my life, a great role model of strength and stability. To my three fantastic children, I love you.

To my senior Pastor, Bishop Melville who is my spiritual covering and mentor, I appreciate and love you. Thank you so much, your tutoring, your living has laid a strong foundational ground in my life. To our dear beloved founder and one of the great pioneers of the gospel, Archbishop Malachi Ramsay thank you dearly for your years of deep revelation teaching that has sincerely impacted my life.

Thank you Rev Pauline Kimba-Smith for your sacrifice in assisting me with this project, I love you, you are a special gift to the body of Christ. Special thanks to all my wonderful friends who have assisted me in the many hours of detail checking and proof-reading.

For all those friends who encouraged me to continue to write and make this project a reality, you know who you are, I really appreciate you. To the Shiloh United Church family your all very special to me, I love you all.

God Bless You

Pastor Beverley Marrett

A Commendation and Blessing

I am incredibly grateful to my heavenly Father for giving me such a wonderful daughter, and woman of God. I know I am undoubtedly blessed, and I am very proud to write this commendation on behalf of Beverley. I thank God for her husband also who is an anointed vessel of the Lord that God is using. I also have other children who are blessed with different gifts.

Ever since my daughter was a small child there was this godliness about her. *She is a person who would always pray, from her school years through college until this day. Beverley is a prayerful person.* I am not surprised that God would use her to produce this book of prayers. I know that her heart, mind, body and spirit is connected to the Lord and *she hears the voice of God speaking to her.*

My daughter has always been a blessing from heaven above to me, her mother, the church and the ministry God has called us to oversight. This is no sugar-coated talk. *This is first-hand knowledge.* Beverley is a person who is highly favoured and connected to God. Just like Mary the mother of Jesus pondered those sayings in her heart about her son, Jesus, I have also pondered over her lifestyle as I watched her growing up.

Everyone who uses this book, and prays these prayers, will experience power from heaven above that will break up the kingdom of darkness from over your life, *your family, your Church and it will bring* divine blessings of God to you, your family *and your Church.*

Congratulations! Pastor Beverley, you are a chosen, set apart and committed vessel of obedience and prayer that the Lord is using mightily in our church. You are a real prayer model!

God Richly Bless and Keep You!

Rt. Revd. L Melville
Presiding Bishop of the Shiloh United Church of Christ Apostolic Worldwide

Introduction

It is strange how some things come about. This project emerged by a simple request from my Bishop (senior Pastor). I was asked to compose some prayers specifically for our 40th Annual Holy Convocation which was held in July 2006. I was excited about the challenge. A team of us got together and completed the task. I thought that was it. I was wrong. The Lord instructed me to go on a 40 day fast prior to all the prayers being written which I now know was part and parcel of him cleansing and preparing me for this venture.

In my sleep, I was awakened with ideas for prayers. In church, my thoughts were interrupted by the Holy Spirit with themes and thoughts for further prayers. This went on until I was persuaded by dear friends to write them down and compile them into a book.

So here it is. 40 prayers of victory. I believe these prayers have been packaged and designed by the Holy Spirit and will help many people and churches who may be struggling and experiencing some of these issues.

The Bible declares in James 5: 16

"The effectual fervent prayer of the righteous man availeth much"

"Pray without ceasing- 1 Thessalonians 5:17

"Men ought always to pray" – Luke 18:1

"Praying always with all types of prayer and supplication for all saints" – Eph 6:18

The Bible declares in Matt 12:11 "And from the days of John the Baptist until now the Kingdom of heaven suffereth violence and the violent take it by force".

Our church is experiencing the power of God moving things visible and invisible and God's delivering power is being manifested as a result of consistent and fervent bible based anointed prayers.

My sincere prayer and earnest desire is that each one of us will be challenged today to obey the voice of the Holy Spirit to go deeper into prayer, and experience the victory we are entitled to in the Name of Jesus.

If this book is a blessing in your life, your ministry, your local church, your home, your loved ones, then please contact me via email at Bev.marrett@btinternet.com or alternatively write to the address at Shiloh United Church Ministries, 8 Gower Street, Burngreave, Sheffield , S4 7JW. Office contact number is 0114 2815997. Our website will soon be available – watch this space. Furthermore if you feel led of the Holy Spirit to sow a love gift into this ministry please send it to the address above and make it payable to Shiloh Church Ministries.

May God Bless You

Pastor Beverley Marrett

How to use this book:

This book can be used in your home as part of your personal prayer and devotion time. Set time aside to read these prayers prayerfully and consistently by faith and you will achieve the desired results, that is victory and breakthrough in your life.

These prayers can also be read corporately involving the whole congregation. This is done by a reader standing out at the front praying the prayers (don't just say them) and allowing the congregation to follow accordingly. These prayers can be used also in small group settings as a pre-cursor to a bible study class or any other meeting.

How to use these prayers:

Step 1: Praise and worship God first. Encourage an atmosphere for the presence of God.

Step 2: Preparation for prayer. Ensure that as a soldier enlisted in God's army you clothe yourself in the whole armour of God. (Ephesians 6: 10-18) .

Step 3: Use the contents page to select the prayers that the Holy Spirit is guiding you to pray.

Caution: May I encourage you that if you have not accepted Jesus Christ as your personal Lord and Saviour to do so now. There is a section for receiving Jesus that you can turn to and receive Him right now. Don't delay. He loves you.

Receiving Jesus Christ

An Invitation to Salvation

It is my sincere hope that if you are reading this book and not yet saved, that you would accept the Lord Jesus Christ today and be saved from the wrath to come and have the hope of eternal life. If you do not know Jesus Christ and want to, then please pray this prayer:

Prayer for Salvation:

Heavenly Father, I come in the Name of Jesus Christ of Nazareth Your Son. I thank you that your Word says in Romans 10:9-10 *"If you acknowledge and confess with your lips that Jesus is Lord and in your heart believe that God raised Him from the dead, you will be saved.* Verse 10 says *"For with the heart a person believes and so is declared righteous and with the mouth he confesses (declares openly and speaks out freely his faith) and confirms his salvation. (Amp).*

Father, I do that now. I confess that Jesus is Lord and I believe in my heart that God raised Jesus from the dead. I ask you now to forgive me of my sins and to come into my heart and cleanse me from all my sins. It is written in St John 3:16 "For God so loved the world that he gave his only begotten Son that whosoever believeth in Him should not perish but have eternal life". I receive your love for me now Lord Jesus according to your Word. I choose to renounce all my evil ways and I step into the light of your love and I receive the gift of eternal life right now.

I thank you I am now born again. I am a new person. I am a christian – a child of the Almighty God. I am saved.

I encourage you to join a bible based church now and begin the exciting journey of walking with Jesus. Read your bible daily along with these prayers and tell others about your new found friend Jesus. God Bless You.

Table Of Contents

Introduction	ix
How to use this book:	xi
Identification through Jesus Christ	1
Soberness of Mind	2
Spirit of Accusation	3
Spirit of Pride	4
Spirit of Slander	5
Spirit of Worry	6
Spirit of Jealousy	7
Spirit of Anger	8
The Power of Grace	9
Unity in the Body of Christ	10
Boldness and Access	11
Strength for the Battle	12
The Unfailing Security of the Lord	13
Seek My Face	14
The Glory of the Church	15
Spirit of Lying	16
Breaking Generational Pain	17
Spirit of Patience	19
Prayer of Agreement for Healing	20
Spirit of Opposition	22
Regrouping of demon spirits	23
Spiritual Prosperity	25
Go Through the Gates	26
Betrayed with a Kiss	27
Spirit of Control and Manipulation	28
Spirit of Greed	29
Power Struggle	31
Spirit of Lust	33
Leaving Egypt (the place of bondage)	35
Worship God	36
Christless Sacrifice	38

Spirit of Fear 40
Love Your Enemies.. 41
Clear The Air 43
Spirit of Backbiting and Gossiping 44
Dry Bones, Live 46
Prayer for my children.. 47
Spiritual Bankruptcy... 48
Territorial Spirits 50
Mighty Men, Arise 51

Identification through Jesus Christ

Heavenly Father, I thank you that it is written in Galatians 2:20: $_{(NIV)}$ "*I have been crucified with Christ and I no longer live, but Christ lives in me. The life I live in the body, I live by faith in the Son of God, who loved me and gave himself for me*".

Jesus through your death, burial and resurrection, a new life of faith is now open to me. I no longer have to struggle inwardly like one who belongs to the world to protect my identity, my image, my reputation, and my social status. As a believer, I gladly receive your identification through the faith in accepting Jesus Christ. I reckon myself dead to sin, but alive to God through Jesus Christ our Lord as it is written in Romans 6: 11.

Father, thank you for the perfected work accomplished through Christ on the cross. In Philippians 1:6$_{(NKJV)}$ it states, "*being confident of this very thing, that He who has begun a good work in you will complete it until the day of Jesus Christ*". According to Your Word in Colossians 2:10$_{(NKJV)}$ it declares that, "And *you are complete in Him (Christ), who is the head of all principality and power*".

It is also written in 2 Corinthians 5: 17:$_{(NIV)}$ "*Therefore, if anyone is in Christ, he is a new creation; the old has gone, the new has come*". I am indeed in Christ and Christ is in me. Joy is available to me now, peace is available to me now, love, blessing, prosperity, and power over sin is available to me now through Christ Jesus.

Father, I thank you for the victory now in Jesus Name. Amen

Soberness of Mind

Heavenly Father, in the Wonderful Name of your Son Jesus Christ of Nazareth, the Anointed One, I thank you that Your Word instructs me in the book of Romans 12:1-2: *(NKJV)* *"I beseech you therefore, brethren, by the mercies of God, that you present your bodies a living sacrifice, holy, acceptable to God, which is your reasonable service. And do not be conformed to this world, but be transformed by the renewing of your mind, that you may prove what is that good and acceptable and perfect will of God".*

I boldly believe and confess that I have the mind of Christ, and no weapon formed against me shall prosper as it is written in Isaiah 54:17. It is also written in 1 Peter 1: 13: *(NIV)* *"Therefore, gird up the loins of your mind, be sober, and rest your hope fully upon the grace that is to be brought to you at the revelation of Jesus Christ".*

Father, in Ephesians 6: 13-17; I am instructed to put on the whole armour of God and place upon myself the helmet of salvation to guard my mind against the attacks of the enemy. I recognise that my thoughts need to be focussed on Christ to have real peace of mind. In Philippians 4:7 *(NKJV)* it states, *"And the peace of God, which surpasses all understanding, will guard your hearts and your minds through Christ Jesus".*

I ask you Father to keep my mind from wandering, daydreaming, indecisiveness and evil fantasies. I reject and bind every thought sent to distort and misguide me, and I release the power of a sound mind, peace, love and obedience in my life. I declare *"God has not given me the spirit of fear, but of power, and of love and of a sound mind".* (2 Timothy 1:7, NKJV)

Father, I thank you for the victory now in Jesus Name. Amen.

Spirit of Accusation

Heavenly Father, I thank you that it is written in Revelation 12:10: (NIV) *"Then I heard a loud voice in heaven say: Now have come the salvation and the power and the kingdom of our God, and the authority of his Christ. For the accuser of our brothers, who accuses them before our God day and night has been hurled down".*

Father, we rebuke and bind the spirit of accusation that Satan sends to weaken and pull apart the saints. Spirit of accusation, I pull you down. I render your working ineffective now. I destroy all the demons sent on assignment against the believers in the body of Christ. I use the precious blood of Jesus Christ to cancel and annihilate all the cell groups, all the satanic cliques and sects formed and created by the enemy.

Any demon holding up the banner of accusation for the weak minded saint to follow, we pursue you and beat you down to dust as it is written in Psalm 18 v 37 and 42. I use the fire of the Holy Ghost to consume my foes on every side as it is recorded in Psalm 97: 3:

Father, thank you that I have the victory over the enemy through the blood of the Lamb, and by the Word of my testimony according to Revelation 12:11.

Father, I thank you for the victory now in Jesus Name.

Amen

Spirit of Pride

Heavenly Father, I thank you that it is written in Isaiah 14:12-14: *"How are you fallen from heaven, O Lucifer, son of the morning! How you are cut down to the ground, you who weakened the nations! For you have said in your heart; I will ascend into heaven, I will exalt my throne above the stars of God; I will also sit on the mount of the congregation, on the farthest sides of the north; I will ascend above the heights of the clouds, I will be like the Most High".*

Father, the evil spirit of pride will cause us to fall from our spiritual rank and position like Lucifer. Every spirit of pride, rebellion, self-will and idolatry dwelling within me, I repent and cast down now. Father, grant me the wisdom to reject every thought of pride and to reject every opportunity to operate in the area of pride.

It is also written in Ezekiel 28:1-3: (NKJV) *"The Word of the Lord came to me again, saying, Son of man, say to the prince of Tyre, Thus says the Lord God: Because your heart is lifted up, and you say I am a god, I sit in the seat of gods, In the midst of the seas, Yet you are a man, and not a god, though you set your heart as the heart of a god".*

Humility creates power in the spiritual realm to overthrow, defeat and resist the power of the kingdom of darkness; I therefore put on the cloak of humility.

Grant me the grace heavenly Father, to humble myself as your Word declares in James 4: 10: (NIV) *"Humble yourselves before the Lord, and he will lift you up".*

It is also written in James 4: 6: (NIV) *"But he gives us more grace. That is why Scripture says: "God opposes the proud but gives grace to the humble".*

Father, I thank you for the victory now in Jesus Name.
Amen

Spirit of Slander

Holy Father in the precious Name of your Son Jesus Christ of Nazareth; I thank you that it is written in Galatians 5:15:(NIV) *"If you keep on biting and devouring each other, watch out or you will be destroyed by each other."*

Father, you have given us exceeding great and precious promises that by these, we have the opportunity to become partakers of the divine nature of Jesus Christ, as it is written in 2 Peter 1:4.

That divine nature rejects the opportunity to slander each other. That divine nature rejects the opportunity to gossip. That divine nature rejects the opportunity to accuse. I desire the best that life can give from the Lord Jesus Christ.

Father, every thought sent from the kingdom of darkness to tempt me to speak evil rather than good; In the Name of Jesus Christ, I cast down those thoughts and I speak God's Word that declares in the book of Titus 3:2:(NIV) *"To slander no-one, to be peaceable and considerate, and to show true humility towards all men"*. It is also written in *Psalm 140:11:*(NKJV) *"Let not a slanderer be established in the earth"*. I confess I will slander no one; I will be peaceable and considerate and show true humility towards all men.

Holy Father, let good things flow from my mouth. It is written in Ephesians 4:29:(NIV) *"Do not let any unwholesome talk come out of your mouths, but only what is helpful for building others up according to their needs, that it may benefit those who listen"*.

Father, I thank you for the victory now in Jesus Name. Amen

Spirit of Worry

Heavenly Father, I thank you that it is written in Matthew 6:25, 28 & 31:(NIV) *"Therefore I tell you, do not worry about your life, what you will eat or drink; or about your body, what you will wear. Is not life more important than food, and the body more important than clothes? ...And why do you worry about clothes? See how the lilies of the field grow. They do not labour or spin. Yet I tell you that not even Solomon in all his splendour was dressed like one of these. So do not worry, saying, "What shall we eat? Or what shall we drink? Or what shall we wear"?*

Father, teach me to trust you and develop that confident faith that does not doubt or question your Word. Your Word commands me in St John 14:1:(NIV) *"Do not let your hearts be troubled. Trust in God; trust also in me".*

Every stronghold of worry and doubt sent to attack my mind in an attempt to destabilise and distract me, I command its power to be broken. I use the Sword of the Spirit to limb down every stronghold and attack. I render the power of worry and doubt powerless now in the Mighty Name of Jesus Christ. I stand on the Word of God that declares in Philippians 4: 6 & 7:(NTL) *"Don't worry about anything; instead pray about everything. Tell God what you need, and thank him for all he has done. Then you will experience God's peace, which exceeds anything we can understand. His peace will guard your hearts and minds as you live in Christ Jesus".*

In the Name of Jesus, I choose your peace over worry, I choose your joy over worry as it is written *"You will keep in perfect peace all who trust in you, all whose thoughts are fixed on you".* (Isaiah 26:3:(NIV))

Father, I thank you for the victory now in Jesus Name. Amen.

Spirit of Jealousy

Heavenly Father in the powerful Name of our Lord Jesus Christ of Nazareth; I thank you for your Word. It is written in Ezekiel 8:3-5:(NIV) *"He stretched out what looked like a hand and took me by the hair of my head. The Spirit lifted me up between the earth and heaven and in visions of God he took me to Jerusalem, to the entrance to the north gate of the inner court, where the idol that provokes to jealousy stood".* Then he said to me, *"Son of man, look towards the north. "So I looked, and in the entrance north of the gate of the altar I saw this idol of jealousy".*

Father, the evil spirit of jealousy constantly seeks for a place of position and power. I dethrone this evil, controlling spirit of jealousy from my life now in Jesus Name. This evil diabolical spirit seeking to manipulate and control my actions, behaviour, emotions and moods, I come against you in the powerful Name of our Lord Jesus Christ of Nazareth.

It is written in 2 Corinthians 10:4:(NIV) *"The weapons we fight with are not the weapons of the world. On the contrary, they have divine power to demolish strongholds. We demolish arguments and every pretension that sets itself up against the knowledge of God, and we take captive, I repeat we take captive, every thought to make it obedient to Christ".*

By the power of the blood and the Name of Jesus Christ, I uproot, I destroy and scatter all devilish plans for my life. The bible declares in Matthew 18:18:(NIV)

"I tell you the truth, whatever you bind on earth will be bound in heaven, and whatever you loose on earth will be loosed in heaven". Right now Satan, I bind and reject the evil spirit of jealousy sowed in my life.

I loose now the power of God's love, his peace, good thoughts, soundness of mind, over my mind and my imagination in Jesus Name. I declare that my mind is cleansed and washed by the pure Word of God and his precious blood.

Father, I thank you for the victory now in Jesus Name. Amen

Spirit of Anger

Heavenly Father, in the peace giving Name of our Lord Jesus Christ of Nazareth; I thank you that it is written in Psalm 37: 8:*(NLT)* *"Stop your anger! Turn from your rage! Do not envy others – it only leads to harm".*

I boldly believe and confess that I am a child of God and my life will never be the same again. I choose to walk in God's love and peace. The Word of God declares, *"You will keep in perfect peace all who trust in you, all whose thoughts are fixed on you".* (Isaiah 26:3:*NLT*)

Father, every situation and circumstances that annoys me and causes me to be irritated, help me to develop the divine ability to speak your Word of peace so I may experience victory at all times. Any learned angry behaviour that is not conducive to my spiritual life, I will not continue with any longer. Every situation that stirs up wrong and negative emotions within me, I declare will not have power over my life any more.

Father I confess, at times I lose control all too quickly. It is written in Proverbs 25:28:*(NLT)*. *"A person without self control is like a city with broken-down walls".* Father, show me how to develop the spirit of self-control. I rebuke, bind and cast down every demon spirit of anger. I relinquish your evil hold on my life.

It is written in James 1:19-20:*(NLT)* *"Understand this, my dear brothers and sisters: You must all be quick to listen, slow to speak, and slow to get angry. Human anger does not produce the righteousness God desires".*

Father, I thank you for the victory now in Jesus Name. Amen

The Power of Grace

Gracious Father, I thank you that it is written in Ephesians 2:7-8: *(NLT)* *"So God can point to us in all future ages as examples of the incredible wealth of his grace and kindness toward us, as shown in all he has done for us who are united with Christ Jesus. God saved you by his grace when you believed. And you can't take credit for this; it is the gift from God"*.

Thank you Father for the love you have demonstrated to me by sending your Son Jesus to die for my sins.

It is written in Ephesians 1: 6-7: *(NLT)* *"So we praise God for the glorious grace he has poured out on us who belong to his dear Son. He is so rich in kindness and grace that he purchased our freedom with the blood of his Son and forgave our sins"*. Thank you for adopting me into the family of God. I was so unworthy but you have blessed me with all spiritual blessings and made me to sit in heavenly places in Christ.

It is also written in 2 Corinthians 12:9: *(NLT)* *"My grace is all you need. My power works best in weakness"*. Father remind me that the mighty power of your Grace is more than able to keep me, and is working best in my times of weakness. When I am weak I must employ your Grace. I call the spirit of Grace – Grace, Grace, God's Mighty Grace come now and assist me in this trial; I need your divine and supernatural gift to see me through.

I declare that your grace Lord is sufficient for me. Help me to balance the adversities and challenges of life without collapsing or foiling and teach me to rest in the comfort of your Grace and peace.

Father, I thank you for the victory now in Jesus Name.

Amen

Unity in the Body of Christ

Gracious Father, I thank you that it is written in Psalms 133:1: (NKJV) *"Behold how good and how pleasant it is for brethren to dwell together in unity"*.

Jesus prayed in St John 17: 11 that we (the body of believers) may be one, even as He and his Father are one.

Father, it is also written in Ephesians 4: 11-15: (NLT) *"Now these are the gifts Christ gave to the church: the apostles, the prophets, the evangelists, and the pastors and teachers. Their responsibility is to equip God's people to do his work and build up the church, the body of Christ. This will continue until we all come to such unity in our faith and knowledge of God's Son that we will be mature in the Lord, measuring up to the full and complete standard of Christ"*.

Father, I thank you that the devil is defeated and God is in control. Hallelujah. Jesus is seated at the right hand of the Father praying for us. It is written in St John 17:20 –22: (NKJV) *"I do not pray for these alone, but also for those who will believe in Me through their Word; that they all may be one, as You Father, are in Me, and I in You; that they also may be one in Us, that the world may believe that You sent Me. And the glory, which you gave me I have given them, that they be one just as we are one"*.

Father, I bind and rebuke every assignment of discord, conflict, apathy, competition, evil factions and strife sent from the enemy against the body of Christ, his weapons will not prosper. The Bible states in Isaiah 54:17: *"No weapon that is formed against thee shall prosper;* and it is written also in Matthew 16:18b: (KJV) *"..and upon this rock I will build my church; and the gates of hell shall not prevail against it"*. Christ is the head of the body, which is the Church.

Father, I thank you for the victory now in Jesus Name.

Amen

Boldness and Access

Heavenly Father, I thank you that it is written in Ephesians 3:12:$_{(KJV)}$ *"In whom we have boldness and access with confidence through the faith of Jesus Christ in God"*.

I thank you for this divine, supernatural boldness and access that is available to me as a believer. It is also written in Psalm 118:19-20:$_{(NIV)}$ *"Open for me the gates of righteousness; I will enter and give thanks to the Lord. This is the gate of the Lord through which the righteous may enter"*.

Father, every door you have opened for me shall remain open for me to go through. Every door that you close against the enemy for my sake shall remain closed so that he cannot touch me.

Father, I command that all spiritual doors to my breakthrough be open to me now. The spiritual doors to my family's breakthrough, the spiritual doors to my finances, the spiritual doors to my health and prosperity be open to me now.

It is recorded in Deuteronomy 28:12:$_{(NKJV)}$ *"The Lord will open to you His good treasure, the heavens, to give the rain to your land in its season, and to bless all the work of your hand"*.

Father, I command all the spiritual doors for my spiritual upliftment, benefit, blessing and deliverance be open – open – open – open – to me now through the Powerful, Conquering Name of our Lord Jesus Christ.

I claim all my blessings, every thing that the enemy has stolen, I take it back and command that Satan loose it and let it go now. The Bible declares in Matthew 18:18: $_{(KJV)}$ *"Verily, I say unto you,* "*Whatsoever ye shall bind on earth shall be bound in heaven, and whatsoever ye shall loose on earth shall be loosed in heaven"*.

Father, I thank you for the victory now in Jesus Name. Amen

Strength for the Battle

Kind loving Father, I thank you that it is written in the book of 2 Samuel 22:40:_(NKJV)_ "*For you have armed me with strength for the battle; you have subdued under me those who rose against me*". It is also written in Ecclesiastes 9:11: _(NKJV)_ "*the race is not for the swift or the battle for the strong*".

Abba Father, my Father, sometimes the battle lasts long and I grow weary, but your Word declares in Isaiah 40:29:_(NKJV)_ "*He gives power to the weak; and to those who have no might he increases strength*".

Your Word also declares in Isaiah 42:3 – 4:_(NKJV)_ "*A bruised reed He will not break, and smoking flax He will not quench; He will bring forth justice for truth. He will not fail nor be discouraged, till He has established justice in the earth; and the coastlands shall wait for his law*".

I strongly believe and confess that God is my strength and power and he makes my way complete. As you anointed King David for battle, so anoint me that I may declare, "*For by You I can run against a troop, by my God I can leap over a wall. It is God who arms me with strength; And makes my way perfect. He makes my feet like the feet of a deer, and sets me on my high places*". (Psalm 18:29 & 32&33:_NKJV_)

Father, I reject the bread of discouragement, and the spirit of weariness commissioned by the powers of darkness against me. I put on the whole armour of God that I will be able to stand against the wiles of the devil. I declare Jesus lives in me; he did not fail, neither shall I. I declare "*The One who is in me, is greater than the one who is in the world*". (1 John 4:4:_KJV_)

Father, I thank you for the victory now in Jesus Name. Amen.

The Unfailing Security of the Lord

Heavenly Father, I thank you that your Word declares in the book of 2 Samuel 22:2-3a: (NTL) "*the Lord is my rock, my fortress and my Saviour. My God is my rock, in whom I find protection*".

Kind Father, you are my unfailing security. You will never abandon or forsake me. You will never let me down. There is no failure in you. I can trust in your Name. It is also written in Isaiah 40:8: (NLT) "*The grass withers, and the flower fades, but the word of our God stands forever*".

It is written in Proverbs 18:10: (NIV) "*The name of the Lord is a strong tower; the righteous run to it and are safe*". Father, your names provide comfort and security:

You are Elohim - my creator,
You are El Elyon – the God Most High,
You are El Roi – the God who sees,
You are El Shaddai – the All Sufficient One,
You are Jehovah -Jireh – the Lord will provide,
You are Jehovah –Rapha – the Lord who Heals.
You are Jehovah-Nissi; the Lord my Banner,
You are Jehovah-Shalom; the Lord my Peace,
Jehovah-Raah: the Lord my Shepherd.

Father, it is written in Psalm 91:1-2: (NKJV) "*He who dwells in the secret place of the Most High, Shall abide under the shadow of the Almighty. I will say of the Lord, "He is my refuge and my fortress; My God, in Him I will trust*".

Father, your Word declares in Psalm 46:1-2: (NKJV) "*God is our refuge and strength, a very present help in trouble. Therefore we will not fear, Even though the earth be removed and though the mountains be carried into the midst of the sea*. In verse 7 also it reads "*The Lord of hosts is with us; The God of Jacob is our refuge*".

Father, I thank you for the victory in Jesus Name. Amen

Seek My Face

Holy Father, in the precious name of your Son Jesus Christ of Nazareth; I thank you that it is written in Psalm 27: 8:*(NKJV)*

"When You said, "Seek My face," My heart said to You, Your face, Lord, I will seek".

Father, in Psalm 63:1:*(NKJV)* David said *"O God, You are my God; early will I seek You; my soul thirsts for You; my flesh longs for You in a dry and thirsty land, where there is no water "*. It is also recorded in Psalm 63:8:*(KJV)* *"My soul followeth hard after thee".*

Father let this be the cry of my heart. Let this be the driving passion in my soul that I long to be in your presence seeking your face and not just your hand.

Father, I prophesy and declare that this generation too will cry out and seek your face. Let the young men and young women seek for you. Let the mothers, fathers, aunts, uncles, grandparents begin to seek you. It is written in Psalm 24: 6:*(KJV)* *"This is the generation of them that seek him that seek thy face, O Jacob. Selah".*

It is written in 2 Chronicles 7:14:*(NKJV)* *"If My people, who are called by My name, will humble themselves, and pray, and seek my face, and turn from their wicked ways, then I will hear from heaven, and will forgive their sin, and heal their land"*.

I declare that as we your people pray, seek your face and turn from our evil ways. This generation who disregard and treat your name with contempt, will turn around and begin to seek for you.

We are instructed in your Word that we must pray without ceasing. *(I Thessalonians 5:17)* We pray, earnestly that our nation, our communities, our families, the educational and judicial officials, the government, politicians and this generation will become passionate and desperate for God and his presence.

Father, let our hearts cry these words "Thy face Lord will I seek".

I thank you for the victory now in Jesus Name. Amen

The Glory of the Church

Heavenly Father, in the glorious Name of your Son Jesus Christ of Nazareth; I thank you that it is written in Isaiah 60:1:(KJV) *"Arise, shine for thy light is come, and the glory of the Lord is risen upon thee".*

Father, I thank you that the church will arise, shine and will be radiant with the glory of the Lord. I thank you that the Gentiles shall come to that light and kings to the brightness of thy rising. Your Word goes on to say in verse 4, (KJV) *"Lift up thine eyes round about, and see; all they gather themselves together, they come to thee; thy sons shall come from far, and thy daughters shall be nursed at thy side".*

Father, I thank you that we have the assurance from your word that the church will develop and grow from strength to strength, in spite of fierce opposition. According to your Word Heavenly Father, the abundant wealth of the Sea shall be turned over to us and nations will come with their treasures in Isaiah 60:4-5.

In the book of Isaiah 60: 11:(KJV) it states, *"Therefore thy gates shall be open continually; they shall not be shut day nor night; that men may bring unto thee the forces of the Gentiles, and that their kings may be brought".*

Father, I thank you that the gates of hell shall not prevail against your church. Your word boldly declares *"If God be for us who can stand against us"?* (Romans 8:31:KJV)

We rebuke and bind every satanic attack against the church; though it seems that the church is tossed and afflicted, yet God will arise and display his power and strength. It is written in Isaiah 54:11:(KJV) *"O thou afflicted, tossed with tempest, and not comforted, behold I will lay thy stones with fair colours, and lay thy foundations with sapphires".*

Father, I thank you for the victory now in Jesus Name. Amen.

Spirit of Lying

Heavenly Father, in the holy Name of your Son Jesus Christ of Nazareth; I thank you that it is written in Ephesians 4:25:*(KJV)* *"Wherefore putting away lying, speak every man truth with his neighbour; for we are members one of another".*

Father, it is written in 2 Corinthians 5:17:*(NKJV)* *"Therefore, if anyone is in Christ, he is a new creation; old things have passed away; behold, all things have become new".*

Father, I need your strength and love to surround me when I am in my hour of temptation. In Psalm 51:6:*(NKJV)* it is written *"Behold, you desire truth in the inward parts".* It is also written in Proverbs 12:19:*(NKJV)* *"The truthful lip shall be established forever: but a lying tongue is but for a moment".*

In our Lord's Prayer Jesus taught his disciples to say *"And lead us not into temptation, but deliver us from the evil one".* (Matthew 6:13:*KJV*) Father, deliver and set me free from the evil spirit of lying. Deliver me completely, O God from the carnal tendency to make excuses and lead me in the paths of your righteousness.

Lord, I give you permission to work in my life. Turn me around. Cause me to see that your way is the best way. Lying is a deed of the flesh that only leads to trouble. Deliver me from lying lips and the temptation to use a lie at any time.

It is written in Proverbs 13:5:*(NKJV)* *"A righteous man hates lying.* It is also written in Proverbs 12:22:*(NKJV)* *"Lying lips are an abomination to the Lord, but those who deal truthfully are his delight".* Father, please forgive me, wash me and make me clean. I repent and I turn to you and receive your forgiveness.

Father, I thank you for the victory now in Jesus Name. Amen

Breaking Generational Pain

Heavenly Father in the Conquering Name of our Lord Jesus Christ of Nazareth; I thank you that it is written, *"Therefore, if anyone is in Christ, he is a new creation; old things have passed away; behold, all things have become new". (2 Corinthians 5:17:_{NKJV})*

Father, the spirit of my forefathers and parents of old come against my soul. They come to overwhelm me and intimidate me. There are times Lord, I feel afraid and hopeless against their attacks, but I am strengthened and encouraged by your Word in Isaiah 43: 1b:*(NKJV)* *"Fear not; for I have redeemed you, I have called you by your name; You are mine".*

Your Word also declares in Galatians 3:13:*(NKJV)* *"Christ has redeemed us from the curse of the law, having become a curse for us (for it is written, "Cursed is everyone who hangs on a tree").* I thank you for the liberty in Jesus Christ. I understand that through Christ's death, burial and resurrection, freedom from my past is now available to me.

I boldly confess I am free from my past and I have been freed from every generational curse and cycle through the precious blood of Jesus Christ. It is written *"If the Son therefore shall make you free, ye shall be free indeed".* (St John 8:36: _{KJV}). Jesus Christ gave his life for me over 2000 years ago and I receive salvation, redemption, every benefit that he purchased for me on the cross. It is mine, deliverance is mine, freedom is mine, hope is mine, healing is mine; I receive it all now in Jesus Name.

It is written *"Yet it was our weaknesses he carried; it was our sorrows that weighed him down. And we thought his troubles were a punishment from God, a punishment for his own sins! But he was pierced for our rebellion, crushed for our sins; He was beaten so we could be healed".* (Isaiah 53:4-5:_{NLT})

Father, I choose to renounce every act of disobedience, rebellion, and self-will attitude in my life and I receive by faith the heart that is responsive to the Word of God and the spirit of God.

I boldly declare and confess I will not be afraid to challenge my past and step into my future. The Apostle Paul wrote ..."*forgetting those things which are behind, and reaching forth unto those things which are before, I press towards the mark for the prize of the high calling of God in Christ Jesus*". (Philippians 3:13-14:$_{KJV}$)

Father, I thank you for the victory now in Jesus Name. Amen.

Spirit of Patience

Heavenly Father in the Precious Name of your Son Jesus Christ of Nazareth; I thank you that it is written in James 1: 4:(KJV) *"But let patience have her perfect work, that ye may be perfect and entire, wanting nothing".*

Father when I am impatient, I focus on my agenda, my needs, my wants rather than your will. Acceptance of your will needs to be established in my heart, in Matthew 26:39:(AMP) it states *"not what I will (not what I desire) but as You will and desire".*

The book of James encourages us to, *"Be patient therefore brethren, unto the coming of the Lord. Behold the husbandman waiteth for the precious fruit of the earth, and hath long patience for it, until he receive the early and latter rain. Be ye also patient establish your hearts: for the coming of the Lord draweth nigh".* (James 5:7-8:KJV)

Father, I command the spirits of restlessness, frustration and impatience that tries to take me out of your will and presence, to flee now from my life. I resist you with the Word of God that declares in Psalm 37: 7 & 9b: (NKJV) *"Rest in the Lord, and wait patiently for him; those that wait upon the Lord, they shall inherit the earth".*

Father, I ask that this divine gift of patience develops and comes to full maturity in my life. This precious gift of patience is necessary for tribulation. This precious gift of patience is necessary for suffering. This precious gift of patience is necessary for establishing good relations. This precious gift is necessary for prosperity, it is necessary for strength. I employ this gracious gift now in my life.

I apply the precious truth of God's Word in Revelation 3:10:(KJV) *"Because thou hast kept the Word of my patience, I will also keep thee from the hour of temptation which shall come upon all the world, to try them..."*

Grant me your divine grace to cultivate and develop the spirit of patience, that I may be complete and lacking nothing.

Father, I thank you for the victory now in Jesus Name. Amen

Prayer of Agreement for Healing

Heavenly Father in the powerful, anointed, healing Name of our Lord Jesus Christ of Nazareth; I thank you for the power of agreement. I stand in agreement this day with the Shiloh United Church Prayer Ministries against the demon of illness attacking my life. Father, it is written in Matthew 18:19:(KJV) *"Again I say unto you, that if two of you shall agree on earth as touching anything that they shall ask, it shall be done for them of my Father, which is in heaven"*.

Father, in the precious name of your Son Jesus Christ, we touch and agree concerning this condition in my body now. It is written in Isaiah 53: 4-5:(KJV) *"Surely he hath borne our griefs and carried our sorrows, yet we did esteem him stricken, smitten of God, and afflicted. But he was wounded for our transgressions, he was bruised for our iniquities, the chastisement of our peace was upon him, and with his stripes we are healed"*.

Father, your Word commands in Mark 11: 22-23:(KJV) *"And Jesus answering said unto them, Have faith in God. For verily I say unto you, That whosoever shall say unto this mountain, be thou removed and be thou cast into the sea; and shall not doubt in his heart, but shall believe that those things which he saith shall come to pass; he shall have whatsoever he saith"*.

I declare the Word of healing, complete healing, nothing missing nothing broken healing, divine deliverance, good health, speedy recovery, no relapse, no adverse effects, no death, and no destructive symptoms will have power over my life and body in the Mighty Name of Jesus Christ.

I command the healing power of God to flow upon me now. Any bad report or diagnosis or prognosis, undesirable x-rays, disturbing scans, or tests received by doctors I declare I will not be moved by what I hear or feel, only what I believe. I shall not be afraid. Father, I will believe and stand on your precious Word. No matter how long and how difficult it may seem. I will trust that your love for me is great. The Word declares, "Who hath believed our report?

(Isaiah 53:1$_{KJV}$) I will say I will believe the report of the Lord. Any demon of illness, death and destruction, I cancel and destroy your plans against my life, body, mind and soul. I command the will of God to be done in my life now. His will is, for *"me to prosper and be in good health". (3 John v 2)*

Father, I thank you for the victory now in Jesus Name. Amen

Spirit of Opposition

Heavenly Father in the precious Name of your Son Jesus Christ of Nazareth; I thank you for the Spirit of Truth. It is written in 1 John 4: 6:(NKJV) *"We are of God; he who knows God hears us; he who is not of God does not hear us"*.

Father, as it is recorded in 2 Timothy 3: 8-9:(KJV) that *"as Jannes and Jambres withstood Moses, so do these also resist the truth; men of corrupt minds, reprobate concerning the faith. But they shall proceed no further; for their folly shall be manifest unto all men"*.

Every person that opposes and resists the Word of truth proceeding out of the mouth of God's leaders are men and women of corrupt minds. It is written they shall proceed no further.

I command and declare that thy truth shall pierce their heart and turn them from their folly. I command every evil spirit of opposition working in the lives of believers to be destroyed now and broken from off them. Every demon riding on the backs of saints to pull down what God is building, they shall proceed no further.

Father, your church is constantly under attack from the opposing spirits of darkness. It is written in Matthew 11: 12:(KJV) *"And from the days of John the Baptist until now the kingdom of heaven suffereth violence and the violent take it by force"*. I plead the precious blood of Jesus Christ against the enemies of the truth. I declare they shall proceed no further. I cancel and grind their works to dust by the power of the Name of Jesus Christ and the blood.

Father, I thank you for the victory now in Jesus Name. Amen

Regrouping of demon spirits

Heavenly Father in the Conquering, Victorious Name of our Lord Jesus Christ of Nazareth; I thank you for your Word. It is written in Luke 11:24-26:(NIV) *"When an evil spirit comes out of a man, it goes through arid places seeking rest and does not find it. Then it says, "I will return to the house I left". When it arrives, it finds the house swept clean and put in order. Then it goes and takes seven spirits more wicked than itself, and they go in and live there".*

Father, those old friends, those old places, those old habits, those old memories, those old thought patterns and cycles that the enemy has used against me; I resist and forcefully bind your evil power in the Name of Jesus. I stand on the Word of God that says in 1 Peter 5:8:(KJV) *"Be sober, be vigilant; because your adversary the devil, as a roaring lion, walketh about seeking whom he may devour".* I ask you Lord to help me keep a watch over my life and to guard every entrance of my mind, will and emotions. Father, I command the fire of the Holy Ghost to burn and consume every evil gathering and conference against my life, and my family.

It is written in Isaiah 54:14-15:(KJV) *"In righteousness shalt thou be established; for thou shalt not fear; and from terror; for it shall not come near thee. Behold, they shall surely gather together, but not by me; whosoever shall gather together against thee shall fall for thy sake".*

Father, every demon that roams around and regroups with others, in an attempt to frustrate and prohibit my progress; I declare I will not allow them to recycle or regroup around me or against me again. I set a watch over my spirit, soul, body, my family and my home. I plead the precious blood of Jesus against the enemies of my soul. I declare the weapons of my warfare are not weak, but they are mighty through God to the pulling down of strongholds.

Every door of disobedience, rebellion, unforgiveness, and pride etc, I may have left open to the enemy, I close now. I repent now of every sin. Father, I ask for your forgiveness and invite you now to take full control of my life. I put on the full armour of God, that I may be able to withstand all the evil attacks and wiles of the devil. I command every door, every access point familiar to the enemy about me to remain closed forever.

Father, I thank you for the victory now in Jesus Name. Amen

Spiritual Prosperity

Heavenly Father, in the Prosperous Name of our Lord Jesus Christ of Nazareth; I thank you that it is written in Psalm 66:12:$_{(NIV)}$ *"You let men ride over our heads; we went through fire and water, but you brought us to a place of abundance"*.

Father, I thank you that you have ordained and predestined me to be prosperous. In 3 John v 2$_{(NKJV),}$ it declares, *"Beloved, I pray that you may prosper in all things and be in health, just as your soul prospers"*.

Thank you Father that you desire me to be the head and not the tail. Thank you that you desire me to be the lender and not the borrower. Thank you that you desire *"to make all grace that is every earthly favour and blessing come to me in abundance; so that I may always and under all circumstances and whatever the need be, self sufficient, possessing enough to require no aid or support"*.*(2 Corinthians 9:8:$_{AMP}$)*

It is also recorded in Joel 2: 24-26:$_{(KJV)}$ *"And the floors shall be full of wheat, and the vats shall overflow with wine and oil. And I will restore to you the years that the locust hath eaten, the cankerworm, and the caterpillar, and the palmerworm, my great army which I sent among you. And ye shall eat in plenty, and be satisfied, and praise the name of the Lord your God, that hath dealt wondrously with you, and my people shall never be ashamed"*.

Heavenly Father, thank you that you desire to bless and make your people rich. It is written *"The blessing of the Lord makes a person rich, and he adds no sorrow with it"*. (Proverbs 10: 22$_{NLT}$). I am blessed and highly favoured.

Father, I thank you for the victory now in Jesus Name. Amen.

Go Through the Gates

Heavenly Father, in the Conquering Name of our Lord Jesus Christ of Nazareth; I thank you that it is written in Isaiah 62 : 10:(KJV) "*Go through, go through the gates; prepare ye the way of the people; cast up, cast up the highway; gather out the stones; lift up a standard for the people*".

Father, as Samson removed the gates of Gaza in the book of Judges 16 you have charged me to rise up and defend what is rightfully mine. It is written in Matthew 16: 18:(KJV) "*and upon this rock I will build my church and the gates of hell shall not prevail against it*". Father, your command is: "*Fear thou not, for I am with thee: be not dismayed; for I am thy God: I will strengthen thee; yea I will help thee; yea, I will uphold thee with the right hand of my righteousness*". (Isaiah 41:10:(KJV))

Father, you anointed Samson with supernatural strength to remove the enemies gates, bar and all, so you have anointed me to remove the enemies camp out of my way. Anywhere the enemy has set up his dwelling place, near my house, around my children, around my church etc. I pick up his belongings, bar and all, and remove them out of my way. No gate shall hold me back, no bar, no barrier, no limitation, no fear shall prevent me taking hold of my destiny.

Father, as Samson looked at the gates he perceived these gates were too small to hold him. I receive supernatural, revelation strength in my inner man to perceive that the enemies' attacks on my life are too small to hold me. The enemies' attacks on my finances are too small to distress me; the enemies' attacks against my children, my family members, and my church are too small for me to fail. Hallelujah, Glory, I praise you right now. Give the Lord praise now for the victory.

I declare and decree I will not be held back. I will go forward through the gates in the strength of the Lord.

Father, I thank you for the victory now in Jesus Name. Amen

Betrayed with a Kiss

Heavenly Father, in the Forgiving Name of our Lord Jesus Christ of Nazareth; I thank you for the power of your grace.

Holy Father, in these last days many of us as saints may be betrayed by our mother, father, friend, close relative, so-called brother or sister in the Lord. Those who we considered a real friend or someone who really cared for us.

It is written in Psalm 41: 9:$_{(NKJV)}$ *"Even, my own familiar friend, in whom I trusted, who ate my bread, has lifted up his heel against me"*.

Father, give me the grace to endure the pain of betrayal and treachery. It is written also in Proverbs 27: 6:$_{(NKJV)}$ *"Faithful are the wounds of a friend; but the kisses of an enemy are deceitful.* Your Word commands me to love my enemies and pray for those who despitefully use me.

Your Word also instructs me in Romans 12:20:$_{(NKJV)}$ *"Therefore, if your enemy is hungry, feed him; if he is thirsty, give him a drink; For in so doing you will heap coals of fire on his head"*.

It is written in 2nd Corinthians 12:9:$_{(NKJV)}$ *"My grace is sufficient for you, for My strength is made perfect in weakness"*. Your grace is able to keep me and bring me through every trial and challenge victoriously.

Father, I thank you for the victory now in Jesus Name. Amen.

Spirit of Control and Manipulation

Heavenly Father in the Mighty, Omnipotent Name of our Lord Jesus Christ of Nazareth; I thank you for the Name of Jesus, that at the Name of Jesus every knee has to bow.

Father, I come against every evil spiritual manipulation and demonic stronghold of control in my life and in our church.

Every spirit disguising itself to gain access and control over the weak minded saints and to be deceitfully subtle in their intentions to control; I expose you. It is written in 2 Corinthians 11: 14:(NKJV) *"For Satan himself transforms himself into an angel of light".*

Father, anoint my eyes to see beyond into the spiritual realm to detect the enemy everywhere he shows up.

Father, I thank you that you have released on the earth the bold spirit of Elijah and Jehu to completely wipe out the spirit of Jezebel and all its family spirits. It is recorded in 2 Kings 9: 33:(NKJV) *"And he said "Throw her down". So they threw her down; and some of her blood was sprinkled on the wall, and on the horses; and he trampled her underfoot".*

Just as Jezebel's body was thrown down, so we the church charge down and ruthlessly cast down, and overthrow the demon spirit of Jezebel. We trample its work and power under our feet as Jehu trampled over Jezebel's body with his horse and chariot.

It is written in Isaiah 61: 1:(NKJV) *"The Spirit of the Lord God is upon me, because the Lord has anointed me".* Thank you for the powerful anointing on my life and in our church that will fight and prevail against the evil controlling spirit of Jezebel.

Father, I thank you for the victory now in Jesus Name. Amen

Spirit of Greed

Heavenly Father, in the Holy Name of your Son Jesus Christ of Nazareth; I thank you that it is written in Acts 5: 3-4:(NIV) *"Then Peter said "Ananias, how is it that Satan has so filled your heart that you have lied to the Holy Spirit and have kept for yourself some of the money you received for the land? Didn't it belong to you before it was sold? And after it was sold, wasn't the money at your disposal? What made you think of doing such a thing? You have not lied to men but to God".*

Father, it is also written in 1 Timothy 6: 9-10:(NKJV) *"But those who desire to be rich fall into temptation and a snare, and into many foolish and harmful lusts which drown men in destruction and perdition. For the love of money is a root of all kinds of evil".*

Father, your kingdom is not of this world. This world's appetite is for the lust of the flesh, the pride of life and the lust of the eyes. Your Word instructs me to love not the world, neither the things in the world. (1 John 2:15-16)

Father, the Word of God declares in Matthew 6:24:(NIV) *"No-one can serve two masters. Either he will hate the one and love the other, or he will be devoted to the one and despise the other. You cannot serve both God and Money".* Every Ananias and Sapphira spirit of selfishness, cunning craftiness, greed and dishonesty, which speaks to my mind to hold back my money rather than to give according to the leading of the Holy Spirit; I cast you down right now. I refuse and reject your evil suggestions of greed and selfishness sent from the kingdom of darkness.

It is written in Luke 6:38:(NIV) *"Give, and it will be given to you; A good measure, pressed down, shaken together and running over, will be poured into your lap. For with the measure you use, it will be measured to you."*

Father, help me to develop the faith to believe and trust in your Word concerning the laws of sowing and reaping. It is more blessed to give than to receive. It is written in 2 Corinthians 9: 6-7:_(NIV) *"Remember this: whoever sows sparingly will also reap sparingly, and whoever sows generously will also reap generously. Each man should give what he has decided in his heart to give, not reluctantly or under compulsion, for God loves a cheerful giver".*

Father, I thank you for the victory now in Jesus Name. Amen

Power Struggle

Heavenly Father in the Almighty Name of your Son Jesus Christ of Nazareth; I thank you that it is written in Psalm 62: 11:_(KJV)_ *"God hath spoken once; twice have I heard this; power belongeth unto God".* Father, I thank you that all power belongeth unto you. Satan, I want to point out to you that power belongeth unto God, not to you.

Every struggle for power, position, recognition and influence seeking to overtake my mind, in an effort to cause me to rebel and operate under a spirit of sorcery; I reject you. This evil spirit that speaks to my mind, causing me to be restless if I am not leading, or not being recognized, or not in control, I confront you. I expose this evil work of the flesh and arrest your power now in the Name of Jesus. I plead the precious blood of Jesus Christ over my mind, imagination and thought life. I surrender every area of my unsurrendered will to you Lord. I give to you my hurt, my pain, areas of insecurity and fear. Father, deliver me now from this evil spirit of lusting for power.

It is written in Acts 8:18-20:_(NKJV)_ *"And when Simon saw that through the laying on of the apostles' hands the Holy Spirit was given, he offered them money, saying "Give me this power also, that anyone on whom I lay hands may receive the Holy Spirit". But Peter said to him, Your money perish with you, because you thought that the gift of God could be purchased with money!*

Father, it is recorded in 2 Samuel 15:12:_(NIV)_ *"While Absalom was offering sacrifices, he also sent for Ahithophel the Gilonite, David's counsellor to come from Giloh, his home town. And so the conspiracy gained strength, and Absalom's following kept on increasing".* Every Absalom spirit working in me, and in our church to subtly gain a place of position and influence through deceit. I command this spirit to be caught and hanged in the Name of Jesus.

Father, my mind is constantly being attacked by the attacking forces of darkness. It is written in Isaiah 26:14:_(NIV)_ *"They are now dead, they live no more; those departed spirits do not rise. You punished them and brought them to ruin."* According to your Living Word, let your Mighty Angels bring to ruin all those evil spirits that seek to destroy me. I declare and decree they are now dead, they shall live no more.

Satan, I expose your evil traits and characteristics right now. Each time I listen to you, you seek to poison my mind, and bind me in bitterness. Father, I recognize the need to be cleansed, I repent therefore of this wickedness and I pray God that you forgive the evil thoughts of my heart right now. Wash and cleanse me by your precious blood that was shed for me and I receive your love now Lord.

Father, I thank you for the victory now in Jesus Name. Amen.

Spirit of Lust

Heavenly Father in the deliverance Name of our Lord Jesus Christ of Nazareth; I thank you that it is written in Genesis 39:7-9:(NKJV) *"And it came to pass after these things that his master's wife cast longing eyes on Joseph, and she said, "Lie with me". But he refused and said to his master's wife, "Look, my master does not know what is with me in the house and he has committed all that he has to my hand. There is no one greater in this house than I, nor has he kept back anything from me but you, because you are his wife. How then can I do this great wickedness, and sin against God"?*

Father, no matter the snare the evil one sets for me you will provide a way of escape. Father, give me the spirit like that of Joseph, a pure spirit that will run from the opportunity to sin, rather than run to sin.

I ask you Lord to give me your divine ability and grace to make the right decisions from now on. Let me be wise and select carefully what I will allow before my eyes, my ears and my heart. I rebuke and bind the demon power of lust, uncleanness, immorality and every family member associated with the spirit of lust. I release divine deliverance, holiness and righteousness now in my life. Father, it is written in your Word in 1 Corinthians 3: 16: (KJV) *"Know ye not that ye are the temple of God, and that the Spirit of God dwelleth in you?"*

Every spirit of lust, I have been feeding and breeding through neglect and disobedience of your Word, unclean images, unclean material and unclean conversation, I ask for forgiveness. I need your help. Father it is written in James 1:14-15:(NKJV) *"But each one is tempted when he is drawn away by his own desires and enticed. Then, when desire has conceived, it gives birth to sin, and sin, when it is full-grown, brings forth death".*

Father, I thank you that it is written *"There hath no temptation taken you but such as is common to man: but God is faithful who will not suffer you to be tempted above that ye are able; but will with the temptation also make a way to escape, that ye may be able to bear it".* (*1 Corinthians 10:13:*$_{KJV}$)

Father, I reach out for your help to correct and transform my life today. I receive your love and I thank you for the victory now in Jesus Name.

Amen

Leaving Egypt (the place of bondage)

Heavenly Father, I thank you that your Word declares in Leviticus 26:13:_(NKJV)

"I am the Lord your God, who brought you out of the land of Egypt, that you should not be their slaves; I have broken the bands of your yoke and made you walk upright".

Lord, you have brought me out of my place of bondage that I would no longer be their slave. You have broken the yoke of slavery from off my neck so I can walk with my head held high.

David said in Psalm 27: 6:_(KJV) *"And now shall mine head be lifted up above mine enemies round about me".* Father, you are such a loving Father there is no evil in your personality. In Psalm 84:11b:_(KJV) it says *"no good thing will he withhold from them that walk uprightly".* Father I know you will look favorably upon me, multiplying all my resources as I walk in obedience to your Word by faith.

It is written in Jeremiah 29:11:_(KJV) *"For I know the thoughts that I think toward you, saith the Lord, thoughts of peace, and not of evil, to give you an expected end".* Father, I know at times my faith will be tested while I wait on your divine supernatural provision, but your Word encourages me to be patient and to trust you. It is written in Psalm 62:5:_(AMP) *"My soul, wait only upon God and silently submit to Him; for my hope and expectation are from Him".*

Father, you will be with me and you will not forsake me. You will cause me to have a surplus of things that I will need to clear out the old to make room for the new.

I expect all this and more according to your love and tender mercies towards me.

Father, I thank you for the victory now in Jesus Name. Amen.

Worship God

Heavenly Father in the Majestic and Holy Name of Jesus Christ of Nazareth; I thank you that you are worthy to be praised. It is written in Psalm 95:6:(KJV) *"O come let us worship and bow down: let us kneel before the Lord our Maker"*. It is also recorded in Psalm 96: 6 & 9:(KJV) *"Honour and majesty are before him; strength and beauty are in his sanctuary. O worship the Lord in the beauty of holiness; fear before him, all the earth"*.

Father, because of your amazing love demonstrated to me through the perfected work on the cross by your Son Jesus Christ, I lift my hands in awesome gratitude to you to say "You are worthy Lord". The Word declares that angels and those around the throne say with a loud voice, *Worthy is the Lamb that was slain to receive power, and riches and wisdom and strength and honour and glory and blessing.* (Revelation 5:12:(KJV))

Father, *"Your mercy is great, above the heavens: and Your truth reaches to the clouds. Be exalted, O God, above the heavens; and Your glory above all the earth"*. (Psalm 108:4-5:(NKJV))

Father, it is written in Revelation 7:9-11:(KJV) *"After this I beheld, and lo, a great multitude which no man could number, of all nations, and kindreds, and people and tongues, stood before the throne, and before the Lamb, clothed with white robes, and palms in their hands: And cried with a loud voice saying, Salvation to our God which sitteth upon the throne, and unto the Lamb. And all the angels stood around about the throne and about the elders and the four beasts and fell before the throne on their faces, and worshipped God.*

I worship you Lord; I adore you and I bow before you. I say, Amen: *Blessing, and glory, and wisdom, and thanksgiving, and honor, and power, and might, be unto our God forever and ever.* (Revelation 7:12:(KJV))

Father, with my whole heart, I praise you. I will bless the Lord at all times and your praise shall continually be in my mouth. I thank you Lord for blessing me with all spiritual blessings. You have caused me to ride in the high places. I will tell of your wonderous love. You are great and worthy to be praised. Hallelujah.

Father, I praise you and thank you for the victory now in Jesus Name. Amen

Christless Sacrifice
(The cost of true discipleship)

Heavenly Father in the precious Name of your Son Jesus Christ of Nazareth; I thank you that it is written in Matthew 7: 21-23:(KJV) *"Not every one that saith unto me, Lord, Lord, shall enter into the kingdom of heaven but he that doeth the will of my Father which is in heaven. Many will say to me in that day, Lord, Lord, have we not prophesied in thy name? and in thy name have cast out devils? And in thy name done many wonderful works? And then will I profess unto them, I never knew you: depart from me, ye that work iniquity".*

Father, the enemy wants me to live an empty, religious, and self-filled life; A life that will not bring honour or glory to your Name. A life of complacency and conformity to this world that will cost me nothing. But you sent Jesus to show me the way of true discipleship. It is written in Luke 14:26-27 & 33:(NIV) *"If anyone comes to me and does not hate his father and mother, his wife and children, his brothers and sisters – yes, even his own life – he cannot be my disciple. And anyone who does not carry his cross and follow me cannot be my disciple"* verse 33 says, *"In the same way, any of you who does not give up everything he has cannot be my disciple".*

I recognize that the cost of true discipleship will cost me everything, but the rewards and benefits are great. Letting go of self dependence and forming a new habit of trust can be difficult, but help me Lord to abandon and let go of myself and learn to rely on you. I confess that I can bear no fruit unless I remain in you for I can do nothing without you.

Father, your Word declares in 1 Corinthians 13:1-3:(NIV) *"If I speak in the tongues of men and of angels, but have not love, I am only a resounding gong or a clanging cymbal. If I have the gift of prophecy and can fathom all mysteries and all knowledge, and if I have a faith that can move mountains, but have not love, I am nothing. If I give all I possess to the poor and surrender my body to the flames, but have not love, I gain nothing".*

Father, let me die from my own self governance, my own self desires, and self centered ambitions. Father, I surrender my mind, my will and my life to you. I give you my all. Let me say like Jesus with a true heart "...*not what I will (not what I desire) but as You will and desire*". (Matthew 26:39:$_{AMP}$)

Father, I thank you for the victory now in my life in Jesus Name. Amen

Spirit of Fear

Heavenly Father, in the fearless Name of your Son Jesus Christ of Nazareth; I thank you that it is written in Psalm 27 :1:(NIV) *"The Lord is my light and my salvation, whom shall I fear? the Lord is the stronghold of my life, of whom shall I be afraid?* I thank you that your Word is my comfort and strength when the arrows of fear come against me.

Father, thank you that I can use the power of the Name of Jesus and the blood against every attack. It is written in Luke 10: 19:(KJV) *"Behold I give unto you power to tread on serpents and scorpions, and over all the power of the enemy: and nothing shall by any means hurt you"*.

Father, through the powerful Name of Jesus and the precious blood, I have power over panic attacks, nervousness, anxiety and every spirit linked to fear. It is written in Hebrews 2:14 -15:(NLT) *"Because God's children are human beings – made of flesh and blood – the Son also became flesh and blood. For only as a human being could he die, and only by dying could he break the power of the devil, who had the power of death. Only in this way could he set free all who have lived their lives as slaves to the fear of dying"*.

According to your Word, I have been delivered from the power of fear and death. My life is no longer subject to chains, fetters and bondages of fear. I have been set free, Hallelujah. Father, I take hold of the authority and truth in your Word and I reject every hold of fear the enemy has used to manipulate and control my life. For it is written *"God has not given me the spirit of fear, but of power and of love and of a sound mind"*.(2 Tim 1:7:KJV)

I declare and decree I am no longer a slave to fear. Fear, you don't control me; You are not my master. I command you to leave now in the Name of Jesus. I serve you notice. I am free by the power of God's Word and the precious blood of Jesus.

Father, I thank you for the victory now in Jesus Name. Amen

Love Your Enemies

Kind, loving and eternal Father, I thank you for your love. It is written in Luke 6:35:(AMP) *"But love your enemies and be kind and do good, and lend, expecting and hoping for nothing in return but considering nothing as lost and despairing of no one; and then your recompense will be rich and you will be sons of the Most High, for he is kind and charitable and good to the ungrateful and the selfish and wicked".*

Father, your Word instructs me to love my enemies, to pray for those that despitefully use me and do good to those that speak evil of me. My carnal tendency looks to seek revenge and keep hard and hostile feelings towards those that seek to do me harm, but your Word tells me in 1 Corinthians 13:8:(NIV) *"Love never fails".*

Father, at times it is hard to find the ability to love when I am being slandered and treated badly. It is also written in 1 Corinthians 4:12:(NIV) *"... When we are cursed, we bless; when we are persecuted, we endure it; when we are slandered, we answer kindly. Up to this moment we have become the scum of the earth, the refuse of the world".*

Father, I thank you that tribulation worketh patience. As painful and uncomfortable is persecution and tribulation, it is necessary for spiritual growth. Father, Jesus triumphed over his enemies making an open show of them publicly and defeated all the powers of darkness by triumphing over them at the cross. In Isaiah 53:7:(NIV) *"He was oppressed and afflicted, yet he did not open his mouth; he was led like a lamb to the slaughter, and as a sheep before her shearers is silent, so he did not open his mouth".*

Father, every battle requires a particular strategy. I reject the desire to follow my old feelings of bitterness, self-pity and feelings of hurt and retaliation. On the contrary, the weapons I fight with have divine power to demolish strongholds. When I am confronted with my enemies, let me follow your instruction that is to be silent. *"In quietness and confidence shall be your strength".* (Isaiah 30:15b:(NKJV))

I thank you that it is written in Galatians 2:20:_(NIV) *"I have been crucified with Christ, and I no longer live, but Christ lives in me. The life I live in the body, I live by faith in the Son of God, who loved me and gave himself for me".*

Father, your Word also instructs me to rejoice and be exceedingly glad when men shall persecute me and say all manner of evil against me; I must Rejoice. I command my soul, heart and mind to rejoice. Rejoice, rejoice and again I say rejoice for great is my reward in heaven.

Father, I thank you for the victory now in Jesus Name. Amen

Clear The Air

Holy Father in the precious Name of our Lord and Saviour Jesus Christ of Nazareth; I thank you that it is written in Job 38:12-13:$_{(NIV)}$ *"Have you ever given orders to the morning, or shown the dawn its place, that it might take the earth by the edges and shake the wicked out of it?"*

Father, I command my day to be ordered by the Lord. I command the sun in the sky to shine its light of blessing on me and my family and to reverse every curse placed on it by satan and his cohorts. Every toxic and poisononus substance released in the atmosphere against me, my family, our church, our community by satan and his agents; I use the precious blood of Jesus to nullify and reject every pollution projected into the air. Every poisononus curse and wicked spell I command it to be sent back to its sender.

It is also written in Proverbs 18:21:$_{(NIV)}$

"The tongue has the power of life and death, and those who love it will eat its fruit".

Father, I use my tongue to speak to the morning and the air that I breathe. I speak life into the atmosphere for God's blessing and righteousness to reign down from the heavens. Any natural elements created by God in the air, land or sea, that satan and his cohorts may be using for their evil purposes, we command the Holy Ghost fire to burn and consume all their evil gatherings and works of darkness.

I speak to the dust of the earth, and command the dust of the ground to go and spread itself into the earth and carry out God's perfect will. I command the holy angels to excel in strength and carry out God's mandate, purpose and plan for those who are heirs of salvation. I decree and declare; let the earth be filled with his glory.

Father, I thank you for the victory now in Jesus Name. Amen

Spirit of Backbiting and Gossiping

Heavenly Father in the Holy Name of your Son Jesus Christ of Nazareth; I thank you that it is written in Galatians 5:15:(NIV) *"If you keep on biting and devouring each other, watch out or you will be destroyed by each other"*.

Father, I need your help to root out the carnal seeds of gossiping and backbiting. This evil practice that satan has lured me into accepting is not pleasing to you Lord. This spirit will create only discord, conflict and bring me to spiritual ruin.

Create within me a clean heart O God, and renew a right spirit within me.

Father, every spirit of gossiping and backbiting operating in my life and our church, I arrest now in the name of Jesus. Every carnal and evil practice of interfering into someone else's affairs must stop now. The evil compulsion driving me to investigate people's affairs and break confidentiality and to share privately with others information gathered, is wrong.

Father, it is written in 2 Corinthians 12:20:(NIV) *"For I am afraid that when I come I may not find you as I want you to be. ..."I fear that there may be quarrelling, jealousy, outbursts of anger, factions, slander, gossip, arrogance and disorder"*.

The evil twin sisters, gossip and backbiting are sent to destroy and prohibit one's spiritual growth and progress. Father, I command the Holy Ghost missiles to locate and destroy the evil communication networks and unholy alliances set up by satan and his agents. I command all their evil powers to fall into deep internal confusion now.

It is written in 1 Peter 1:15-16:(NIV) *"But just as he who called you is holy, so be holy in all you do; verse 16 says for it is written: Be holy, because I am holy"*. Father, I want to be holy. Help me to break free from every conversation, soul ties and unhealthy relationships that may be manipulating me, and prevent me also from manipulating others. All the evil seeds of discord and strife sown in my life, and seeds I may have sown in others; I ask you to root them out by the power of your Holy Spirit and cause them to wither and die and not bear fruit. I declare I am coming out and I declare myself free. I thank you that the enemy is under my feet and his power is destroyed now.

Father, I thank you for the victory now in Jesus Name. Amen.

Dry Bones, Live

Father in the Life Giving Name of Jesus Christ of Nazareth; I thank you that it is written in Ezekiel 37:1,3 & 4:(KJV)

"The hand of the Lord was upon me, and carried me out in the spirit of the Lord, and set me down in the midst of the valley which was full of bones.

And he said unto me, Son of man, can these bones live? And I answered, O Lord God, thou knowest.

Again he said unto me, Prophesy upon these bones, and say unto them, O ye dry bones, hear the Word of the Lord".

Father, every dry, barren and unfruitful area within my life, cause your breath to enter into me that I shall live.

Father, I need to come alive to righteousness. Father, I started well, I want to finish well; help me Lord not to die. It is written in Psalm 118:17:(KJV) *"I shall not die, but live and declare the works of the Lord".* I prophesy I shall not die, but I shall live. It is written in St John 10:10b:(NKJV) *"I have come that they may have life, and that they may have it more abundantly".*

I prophesy that I shall come up out of the grave; a place assigned only for the dead, and be reunited in fellowship with my God. It is written in Romans 8:11:(NLT) *"The Spirit of God, who raised Jesus from the dead, lives in you. And just as God raised Jesus Christ from the dead, he will give life to your mortal bodies by this same Spirit living within you".*

Father, I turn aside and reject every act of disobedience, self-will, rebellion, unfaithfulness to you, and I ask for divine forgiveness and I bow in humble repentance.

It is also written in Psalm 23:3:(KJV) *"He restoreth my soul".* Father, thank you, you are restoring my soul right now and will lead me in the paths of righteousness for your name's sake. I repeat and boldly declare; I shall not die, but live.

Father, I thank you for the victory now in Jesus Name. Amen.

Prayer for my children

Heavenly Father, in the precious Name of Jesus Christ of Nazareth; I thank you that it is written in Ephesians 6:1:$_{(KJV)}$ *"Children obey your parents in the Lord, for this is right".*

Father, every demonic seed of rebellion, disobedience, naughtiness sent by the kingdom of darkness to destroy and weaken my children's desire and love for God and his Word. I speak against their evil works and command and decree that all their evil assignments against my children be destroyed now. I release the spirit of obedience, confidence, success, desire for prayer and the things of God upon my children.

I cancel and nullify the spirit of addiction to television, and other time wasting activities that the enemy puts into their minds and before their eyes to enjoy to hinder their progress and development. Father, I also ask that you surround them with godly friends who will create a positive environment for them to maximize their potential.

I declare my children are the head, and not the tail, they are above and never beneath. I apply the precious blood of Jesus Christ over my children now, and ask that your Mighty Angels would follow them wherever they go in Jesus Name.

Father, I bind my children to the things of God, and command that they be loosed from the things of this world that may so easily beset them for it is written in Matthew 18:18:$_{(KJV)}$ *"Verily, I say unto you, "Whatsoever ye shall bind on earth shall be bound in heaven, and whatsoever ye shall loose on earth shall be loosed in heaven".*

Father, I thank you for the victory now in Jesus Name. Amen

Spiritual Bankruptcy

Heavenly Father in the Powerful Keeping Name of our Lord Jesus Christ of Nazareth; I thank you that it is written in Luke 14:28-30:$_{(KJV)}$ *"For which of you, intending to build a tower, sitteth not down first, and counteth the cost, whether he have sufficient to finish it?*

"Lest haply, after he hath laid the foundation, and is not able to finish it, all that behold it begin to mock him,

"Saying, This man began to build, and was not able to finish".

Father, every spirit sent from satan's kingdom to discourage and cut short God's plan for my life will not prevail. Every effort to hinder and foil my progress by satan and his demons will not prosper. I bind and overthrow your evil cohorts and assign God's mighty angels to torment you without relief. My enemies will not mock me because I did not continue the race, I will finish, and I will finish with joy and strength.

Father, keep me from falling into spiritual bankruptcy. The habit of starting then stopping. The habit of saying and not doing. The pattern of moving forward then falling backwards. I bind and rebuke the powers of procrastination and apathy.

Father, it is written in Hebrews 12:2:$_{(KJV)}$ *"Looking unto Jesus the author and finisher of our faith, who for the joy that was set before him endured the cross".*

Father, your Word declares that Jesus is the author and the finisher of our faith. Every thing Jesus starts he finishes. Nothing is left hanging or incomplete. Father, help me to recognise that the finisher is on the inside of me.

It is written also in Philippians 1:6:$_{(NIV)}$ *"Being confident of this, that he who began a good work in you will carry it on to completion until the day of Christ Jesus".*

Father, deliver my soul from spiritual bankruptcy; Deliver my family from spiritual bankruptcy; Deliver our church from spiritual bankruptcy; Deliver my finances from spiritual bankruptcy.

I will declare like the Apostle Paul: *"I have fought the good fight, I have finished the race"*. (2 Timothy 4:7:$_{NKJV}$)

Father, I thank you for the victory now in Jesus Name. Amen.

Territorial Spirits

Heavenly Father in the mighty, Omnipotent Name of our Lord Jesus Christ of Nazareth; I thank you that it is written in Jeremiah 1:10: (NKJV)

"See, I have this day set you over the nations and over the kingdoms;

To root out and to pull down; to destroy and to throw down; to build and to plant".

Father every evil, territorial demonic power working in our church seeking to assert itself; I expose you. Every evil family spirits, soul ties, established by the enemy; I break your power and authority now in the mighty Name of Jesus Christ of Nazareth. I root you out and destroy you. I disconnect you and destroy your sources of reconnection. I sprinkle the precious blood of Jesus Christ and command these territorial spirits to cease from operating in our church and this surrounding area. I command these spirits to be tormented, afflicted and sent back to their sender now.

I command and decree that you have no legal right or position in this church or this locality. You are not in charge of this area or this church. Jesus Christ is the head of this church, he spoiled principalities and powers and made an open show of them.

Leave now, take your family spirits and depart. We, the church serve you notice. Move swiftly out of our way. You have been evicted and removed.

Father, I thank you for the victory now in Jesus Name. Amen

Mighty Men, Arise

Heavenly Father in the deliverance name of our Lord Jesus Christ of Nazareth; I thank you that it is written in Joel 3: 9:(NIV) *"Proclaim this among the nations; Prepare for war! Rouse the warriors! Let all the fighting men draw near and attack"*.

From the time of King Herod, Satan has sought to destroy the male champions and warriors in an attempt to destabilize and weaken man's position in the earth realm.

CONFESS:

Father, I break free from all the shackles, chains, and fetters restricting me. I take authority over satan's power that is preventing me from reaching and achieving my destiny. Every controlling force of fear, selfishness, low self esteem, rebelliousness, hopelessness, anger and lack of love; I reject you and I receive God's mighty power and grace to begin to heal and totally transform me.

Father, it is written in Zechariah 4: 6b(NKJV) *"Not by might, nor by power but by My Spirit says the Lord of hosts"*. The word of the Lord declares in St John 12:32:(NIV) *"But I when I am lifted up from the earth, will draw all men to myself"*. God is preparing his mighty men to take their true position of dominion and authority.

CONFESS:

I declare I will not be silent. I declare I will take my rightful position in the earth realm. I declare I am a mighty man of war. Strength, confidence and courage are my portion. I will arise out of my slumber, out of my sleep through the powerful Name of Jesus and his blood. I put on my military garments for war. I will fight for my life, I will fight for my family, I will fight for my church, and I will fight and stand in the gap for the nations. Jesus has given me the power to stand against all principalities and powers. I will arise and be strong in the Lord and the power of his might and take my position now.

Father, I thank you for the victory now in Jesus Name. Amen.

Printed in the United Kingdom by
Lightning Source UK Ltd., Milton Keynes
139008UK00002B/63/P